Picture A P

By

Diana Butler

ISBN No: 978-1-899499-79-3

Cover and all photographs : Diana Butler

Printed and bound in Great Britain by
The Minster Press,
14/15 Mill Lane,
Wimborne Minster,
Dorset,
BH21 1LN

INTRODUCTION

Welcome to this collection of my poetry
written through the years when inspired
by events or personal thoughts.

Some poems were prompted by events
of great sadness or joy. Others were
written in quiet reflection.

My school and college days encouraged
expression through poetry, music and art.

I grew up in Southampton and moved
to Dorset when I married - never far
from countryside and coast.

Always inspired by travel and nature,
all the photographs are my own,
taken at home and abroad.

I hope you enjoy sharing my thoughts
and perhaps you will relate to some
experiences, views or emotions.

CONTENTS

<u>Understanding</u>

We often fail to see beyond the eyes
Others' faults are easily perceived
But what of their aspirations …
Or are we too busy with ours
To realize that others may dwell
On a different plane?

Time waits to find the one
Who shall grasp its meaning
For who are we to judge others
If the plane we are on
Is not theirs ?

For each must find his own foothold
On the ladder of life
And grasp hold of his understanding
Lest it fly away quickly
Leaving only a glimpse
Of the part of him that passes by

1981

A Part

You play on my thoughts
And in my dreams
You were so much part of me

You were so involved
In your own little world
That you just couldn't see

How we both had our own desires
That we followed in separate ways
You failed to see
What it meant to me
If that little world had been ours

You were like a bird of prey
Soaring to be free
But on the way you landed
And took a part of me

1981

Comfort

You are my one salvation
When all seems too much to bear
You comfort me and give me hope
I'm glad that You are there

Thoughts

I hear my thoughts
When I think at night
For all is quiet
Time no longer measured
My mind can recoil
On the days events

Hope

A glimmer of hope is all you need
To rebuild what you were before
Take heart and be thankful
That you have overcome
Once more

Wonder

I sit here on this stool
And wonder …
How did I come to
Be here at all ?

Lead Me

Perhaps I think too long and too deep
Oft times perplexed at complexities
If only, perhaps, how or why
Lead me back to the same points

As if struggling through a jungle
To be turned back from the prize ahead
Getting caught along the way
Help me know the path to tread

My feet are weary of wandering
Please take me by the hand
And lead me to a better place
To love and understand

Summer 1982

<u>Trees</u>

The forest stands tall and majestic
A refuge for the soul
For here, no-one can harm it
Protected by the pillars of time

They have survived through years
Of plenty and years of few
To stand witness for the years to come

Here the light is filtered
So that life may not be destroyed
A shelter for all dwellers
Whether animal or plant

To live secluded lives
In the company of old friends

1982-3

A Purpose

I feel like a lost soul ...
There's so much to do and see
But sometimes I wonder where
I'm going
Where life is leading me

I'd like to grasp and hold onto something
But just when I think something's there
It dissolves and I am lost again
Clinging to illusive dreams

And yet, when life is mapped out
Everything in regimented order
I feel restricted and programmed
I long for some disorder

The mind is such a realm of mystery
I wonder at my reasoning
Attitudes change as passing days
Alongside changing circumstance

Are moods the result of a restless mind
Or uncertainty of what will be ?
To put one's all into belief
A purpose in life is the key

To tread a path not trodden before
Feels safe and secure in itself
To strive for a purpose
You know is right

The mind will find soul
True wealth

1982

Depths

When the sun is glistening
Upon the majestic sea
Then all my thoughts come rushing
All seems clear to me

I feel the thoughts but cannot grasp
The swell that changes form
There is something seeking refuge
In the patterns of the foam

Each wave holds inner meaning
That brings hope to me
There is something so much stronger
That lies waiting to be freed

But who can solve the secret ?
Perhaps it's never found
The depths remain as stalwart
As the time they covered ground

No words can ever transform it
To be passed by any tongue
Perhaps it's understanding
That the mind is more than form

That somewhere in this ocean
An answer can be found
It does not make me anxious
But fills me with strange calm

For who's to say that one day
When I look upon the sea
The depths that strengthen feeling
Will set my spirit free

1980s

Little Bird

The bird sings his tune of happiness
Calling others to join with him
For it is the beginning of a new day
All that was sung yesterday
Will be the madrigal of today

Soul

The soul that finds no comfort
Is forever searching for itself
If only in the refections of others

If then it does not find itself
Perhaps it has travelled too far
And passed itself along the way

1980s

19

Athens to Gatwick

Craggy peaks rising from velvet depths
Snow nestled in pockets and crevices
Clashing arêtes forming
Menacing contours

Wisps of cloud hang above the peaks
While all around a hazy calm
Of watery rose and blue

These bold peaks give way to softer
Lower forms, clad in mossy green

On to lowlands of patchwork
Beige and green
And vast expanses ornamented with
Pink and white towns and
Scribbled roads

Towns like nuclei amid shades of green
Pink beige patches on a softly
Undulating land
Seem like ordered amoebae
Resting on a quiet dark land
Each splays tendrils to reach outer limits

A mystical stillness of greys and whites
Forming illusions of snowscape
Caverns seem to lay open
As wisps of cloud float over
More cumulative layers below

Grey furrowed masses tainted
As if by smoke
Looking into the blue pools formed
Sense of perspective is lost
There are no harsh angles in such
A changing world of vaporous motion

August 1984

21

Noar Hill

The fence was beginning to shape up
With wire held in place to be pulled up
Members strained at the end
let's get rid of the bend
Before long the wire had moved up

One slack at the end was the next bend
The next bend pulled tort by the wrench,
then
A shout and a ping
Now you've ruined the thing
So we'll have to start over again then

Why have wire and wood
in the first place ?
Said the one with the wrench
and a red face
Wood's much better spliced
But more heavily priced
So let's try it again but at **my** pace

The wire was pulled to perfection
This time to the adequate tension
Just fix into place
And we're ready to face
The next section
But **you** can do that one!

12 November 1984

Inspired by a volunteer conservation task in Hampshire.
The details are purely fictitious.

<u>Sea</u>

Water can take on many moods
It can be calm and gentle
Crystal clear so that the jewels
In its bed show their riches

It can be playful or tease
With its dancing horses
Each releasing white foam
That fizzes then falls

It can be powerful and dominant
Letting nothing disturb its swell
Rolling to the shore
And sucking up pebbles
To spit out the surplus on return

It chooses its time to conquer
Showing no mercy, raging and dark
To carry off anything it its way
Nothing can halt its path

Perhaps mankind can be likened to the sea
Changeable or steadfast, hiding his moods
To appear, perhaps
As the onlooker wants him to seem

<u>Destiny</u>

Life is a long road we tread
Picking up experience and knowledge
as we go
Sometimes we find it difficult to reach
And secure the things we need

Opportunities and pleasures may appear
From nowhere and do not have to be
sought
Sometimes we wander aimlessly
Not really sure of what we are looking for

Opportunities may lay before us but either
We do not see them or cannot grasp them
As we are, at that moment
In the wrong place or time

We may be distracted along the way
And forget what we are seeking
Or change our minds
About the importance of such

Our distractions may be beneficial
Or may delay our progress
When reaching the crossroads
We might not know which way to turn

We may stay there until something
Picks us up and carries us on
We may turn one way and
Not like where we are going

We may go straight on with purpose
And determination to achieve
We may find another direction is easier
And quicker to bring us to our destination

We may turn so many ways that we lose
ourselves
One thing remains constant ….
It is our decision as to our chosen route
Destiny has planned our ultimate
destination

June 1984

<u>Epilogue</u>

She said her life was like a book
She thought of it in chapters
Her childhood, school and then the war
Her marriage, family and work

She accepted that her life would end
But sat composed and spoke her thoughts
She told me of her husband's end
Now resident in a mental ward

Disregarding her own painful state
Her main concern was for him
That with the money she would leave
He'd be cared for ~ to the end

20 January 1986

Judith Piper - an inspiring lady I nursed in hospital.

Beauty

Beauty ~ as inner self
Is in the eye of the beholder
Hidden beauty may be discovered
But equally, may be created
If that is what the beholder desires

Realms

Each man lives within his own realm
Not all realms can be entered by another
Especially if one is not welcomed

Realms can be shared but not completely
As no man can live in another's mind
Or share his spirit

1980s

30

Get Out

Life is too precious to let pass by
Without first stopping to wonder why

There are so many people
In this world to meet
Whether out in the country
Or down in the street

So don't go around
With your head underground
Somewhere out there
Friends can be found

20 January 1986

Music

Music is the language of the world
For in it and through it we are able
To share and communicate what we feel
Without restriction of word or grammar

It touches the heart in a subtle way
We cannot describe the emotion
As sometimes a note is all that's required
To awaken feelings forgotten or new

Smile

A smile is such a friendly thing
A sign that we all share
It breaks the barriers down at once
More comfortable than a stare

Packing 1986

Sorting, stacking, wrapping, packing
So many things to sort
Old things, new things
Those "that will do" things
And some things yet to be bought

Full Moon

The moon casts out its brilliant light
Brightening the sky on this clear night
So all our friends can share the sight
Of fireworks, bonfire and starry night

Love

Love is the need
To love someone completely
To explore the hidden realms
Of the mind
And share in the freedom
Of the spirit

Listen

Why chain yourself
To your own beliefs?
Listen to your neighbour
For he may have been
Where you have not

<u>Expecting Rain</u>

The sky hangs grey with dampness
Birds sing unseen from the trees
The air is heavy and still

The breeze cannot be heard
But its presence is seen
By the movement of the fir

Seeming weary and reluctant
It moves with lumbering stance
An air of great expectance
As we await the oncoming shower

1986

Longing

You make me feel so happy
In the things you say and do
Everywhere we go together
Though familiar , I see anew

Walking in natural places
Where both of us feel we belong
Watching the seabirds and people
Listening to music and song

This time should last forever
But you have to leave and go on
I wish you could stay forever
As with you I feel really strong

Why must the good times pass quickly
Why does the bird sing his song
Why do the people that matter
Stay here and then they are gone ?

30   July 1986

Stanthorpe

This land of space and plenty
Holds sights for all to see
But what little pleasure some get here
They're not where they want to be

Some move from place to place now
Working wherever they can
The boss isn't easy to please
How can this be a life for a man ?

Some towns fill their bars with drifters
Not always at home with the place
Once drunk, he swears at the locals
This time he's escaped with his face

It's due to the landlord's handling
Of situations before they get rough
Tells them straight without any rambling
"Now shut it - I've had enough"

Australia   20 December 1986

Stanthorpe II

"Wanna game of pool" ?
As he stands from his stool
And checks my beer's not empty

50 cents on the table
Balls set up and we're able
To break and start the game

It's not always easy
To pot slick and sleazy
Just shoot and hope for the best

Although I'm no good
Company's all that it should
With tips on how to direct the cue

He's potted the black
I was much further back
"Good game … d'ya wanna nother" ?

20 December 1986

39

Girls on a See-Saw

Up and down, hit the ground
This see-saw's a sharing thing
For one on her own
Would just sit and groan
Why can't I go up on my own ?

Girls on Swings

To and fro, here we go
Swinging in the sun
Me in mine, you in yours
Aren't we having fun

Bicycle

This bicycle goes faster than foot
Whether good or ill
But both slow down together
When we try to go uphill

Tenterfield - Australia   20 December 1986

Tenterfield

As we walk through the park
What's that tree and that bark ?
The scent of something unfamiliar

Can't name a bush
A tree or a flower
But step lightly
We may see some fauna

Colourful birds are often seen
Along with their unusual cry
The lizards are quick to dart away
Before we can identify

Sometimes a rustle is heard ahead
But too far to see what it is
Our senses are tuned with every step
To the park in its natural splendour

20 December 1986

Going Away

What a day to be going away
Leaving my new friends
But there's much to see and do
In a life that too quickly ends

Blue & Green

Blue and green should never be seen
But sky and leaf go together
Whoever said that must be blind
For it's harmonised with the weather

Town

Cars, bars, shops and stops
Are all part of a town
But people and parks make a town
From a dwelling into a home

Tenterfield - Australia   20 December 1986

Narooma Oyster Beds

Sitting amid the quiet of day
With nothing to do and nothing to say
My senses have a while to breathe
To take account of all around

The shells are minutely formed
The tide now low, with faint of sound
Caressing the shore of shell and sand
The oysters here are plentifully found

The sky turns from a blue to grey
As light fades with the end of day
The breeze that earlier beat the trees
Now calmed to still, no rustling leaves

The seaweed swept upon the shore
Like strings of beads and many more
Are washed beneath the surface clear
Like hair, cleaned in the flow, so near

NSW 1987

<u>Travelling</u>

Here we are just travelling through
All in search of something new
Places to be and people to see
But most of all, the desire to be free

Free from role and accountability
No routine or philosophy
Some have things they want to forget
Others want to experience jet

Families, friends or those on their own
Heading somewhere
They're not yet known
Apprehension, excitement and curiosity

But most of all
The desire to be free

New Zealand - 15 March 1987

Spanish Blues

My friend you are so far away
I wish you could come here to stay
For I've lost my way without you
Things here seem so grey

To share the sights and sounds
In the country or the city
Our time together always short
Filled with words of such import

Why did consequence bring us together
Will I have to wait forever
To be loved by you completely
Or must I continue to love discretely

1987

Rufus Stone

The beech rise gracefully skyward
Their smooth bark gentle on the eye
To sit amid the calming hues
Of green and bronze
That soothe the mind and fill the heart

Birds and breeze together sing
The tapping woodpecker
Chaffinch on the wing
A robin calling his distant mate
Flies free - while I sit here
And contemplate

New Forest 8 April 1988

<u>Self</u>

Depression gives depth to feeling
Bringing you closer to your 'self'
Don't be afraid to discover
The reasons
For feeling the way you do

Put your feelings into words or art
Straighten out your hazy thoughts
For convention teaches us inhibition
Which hides the truth
And confuses purpose

For recognition of self gives strength
An inner force no man can own
It's yours to support you
Through dark days
Discover your self
And you're not alone

You have to face up to what you are
Give yourself credit where it's due
Nobody is perfect
So work on your strengths
Your spirit will carry you through

Each person has something to give
A skill, a thought or a wit
Don't judge yourself against standards
Of wealth, status, power and ego

These mean nothing in real terms
Of happiness, health and fulfilment
Through dark days
Comes understanding of self
And your part in life

12 June 1990

Sundown to Kymh

The soft sea air wafts through my hair
The sun's hot rays bathe my skin
My thoughts pass by without a care
The soothing of the soul within

Whisked white foam
And fresh tossed spray
Petrol blue ocean
On a clear azure day

Soft crags rising
From a gently lapping bed
Clad in green
Steep slopes to the shore

Changing light upon the sea
Brings deeper colour to the blue
Bulky islands fade in two dimension
Delicate shades of purple hue

Distant hills obscured by haze
Greyish blue on a clear hot day
Nestled in a sky of infinite blue
Shore, sea, hills and changing views

June 1991

Autumn

Watery sunlight through the trees
Falling leaves on softer breeze
Gold and russets in upper reaches
Copper adorns the graceful beeches

Rustling leaves that dance along
Chaffinch sings his zealous song
Now seen clearly against the sky
Woodland birds on branches high

Mossy cushions of velvet green
Webs that glisten with dewy sheen
Bright coloured fungi among the leaves
And skeletal lichen on the trees

Squirrels gather their vital store
In time for winters cold, once more
Ponies coats now thick and warm
Pigs at pannage search out acorns

Deer that graze in quiet glades
As the daylight gently fades
Colours in their warmer range
Natures time for rest and change

Art Gallery

Quiet footsteps on polished floors
Paintings hung on pale walls
People move without much sound
Respecting others and those around

Seeing the colour and the form
Stopping to ponder on those that dawn
Absorbing the essence when
understanding
The message sent out in certain paintings

A closer look at technique and style
Those that please or make you smile
Others that threaten or confuse
Are quickly passed without further muse

Perhaps returning to favourite paintings
Checking names or certain dating
Leaving inspired with lifted soul
Understanding and feeling whole

11 June 1994

Christmas

Christmas is a time of cheer
Making good before New Year
People come from far and near
Spending time with those held dear

Good wishes from friends, new and old
Warm the heart amid the cold
We remember the story told, of Jesus
Frankincense, myrrh and gold

Just as gifts were laid before
We bring gifts and smile once more
A child was born for us to live
To love each other and forgive

Sept 1994

Snowdrops

Through the frozen earth they peep
Slowly from their winter sleep
Slender green they push their way
Up towards the light of day

Purest white in upright duty
Lowered heads conceal their beauty
Delicate lines enrich the petals
Protected from the frost that settles

Shining bright in joyous crowds
Under trees and over mounds
Brilliant white they greet the day
Spreading beauty along the way

2005

Car Trouble

Cars are wonderful things, until
You're stuck on green and sitting still
You were on your way home
But now not very sure
"If this thing will last out
Just a few minutes more"

You're cursing and praying
That somehow, some way
It'll creep just far enough
To avoid congestion
"To be stuck in the middle lane"
Can't risk the thought
Your brow now tense
And you ignore the suggestion

"Don't stop in front of me
Please let me pass"
This thing might get there
If not very fast
One more roundabout, nearly there
Car and I tottered home on a prayer

1996

58

In Our Hearts

Life is cut short
We don't know why
Turn over our thoughts
And frequently cry

The loss of a friend
So dear and such fun
Why did it happen
To someone so young

We question the purpose
Of a life quickly taken
We search for an answer
But remain deeply shaken

Our only strength
Is drawn from each other
We meet up and hug
And hope we'll recover

You were our friend
Now gone from our grasp
A wife and a mother
Dearly loved now and past

We remember with joy
Your smile and laughter
You remain in our hearts
Today and forever

7 November 2000

The Child Within

Never lose the child within
She speaks with freedom
And thinks with clarity

She is curious to learn
And express her feelings
Joy frustration and
Excitement abound

Sharing new games
And treasuring toys
Running as fast as she can
With the boys

Collecting blossom
And dandelion fairies
Making rose petal perfume
And chains of white daisies

Mud pies in the garden
And tea in the wigwam
Collecting shells and pebbles
Making castles of sand

Feeding popcorn to giraffes
And watching seals swim
Laughing at monkeys
And the penguins

She creates and imagines
A world full of pleasure
A world to discover
And play in forever

22 March 2003

Song For Nick

You taught us how to sing
With open arms and heart
You taught us how to sing
With each and every part

You are our inspiration
That stirs creative thought
That earth and man and nature
Are all as one …

5 Feb 2014

Written with thanks and in memory of
Nick Prater.
A great composer, singer and
Natural Voice tutor.
These are the words to my song of harmony
" Song For Nick "

Secret Wish

Wishing for a world
Without war and oppression
No need for enforcement
Or political repression

Wishing for a world
Where people can be free
From target driven culture
That stifles creativity

Wishing for a world
That values individuality
Potential that is realised
Independence a reality

Wishing for a world
That recognises nature
Can protect and can provide
If treated as a mentor

Wishing for a world
Free from ego and aggression
Working together to protect
No need for domination

Wishing for a world
That cherishes our time
The gift of life and freedom
This secret wish is mine

2 August 2015

<u>Searching</u>

Searching for something
Just beyond grasp
Glimpse a moment of clarity
Before it is past

Something to give
And something to take
Experience and skills
New ideas when you wake

Trying so hard
To open the doors
Busy with work
With little time to pause

Too much to consider
Wonder which direction
Strive to achieve
Life's ultimate perfection

Time for reflection
Let chance come your way
Go out and discover
You have something to say

29 July 2015

Written for a close friend

Dear Cat

I hold you close
And stroke your fur
You feel secure
I hear your purr

Your tone is steady
The vibration strong
You feel my love
We have a bond

You stay with me
When I'm not well
You understand
No need to tell

I hold you dear
With all my heart
Your wildness treasured
From the start

18 October 2015

Picnic

Meet in the park
With happy heart
We'll share some verse together

Some wine and juice
But no roast goose
We'll carry from the car

Some bread and cheese
And salad please
We'll add some dips and cake

Get out the rug
I've brought the mugs
We're going to have a feast

30 August 2016

Tribute to Candy Cat

You chose us from the start
And captured both our hearts
Keen for us to take you home
We picked you up without a moan

The lady had left you overnight
You were so pleased to reach sunlight
So on the carpet you rolled and purred
And settled into our small world

You liked our hugs and created games
Learning quickly reflections and names
Hooking out books from the shelves
Hide and seek, rubber mouse and pencils

You learned from squirrels how to climb
You watched TV for quite a time
You dived on sheets and dashed around
Could jump full circle from the ground

You brought in birds and mice for play
The blue tit survived and flew away
You learnt that birds were wrong to catch
So ambushed us on morning watch

We called you Candy
with stripes and tufts
Spotted belly and ginger spot
You enriched our lives
with affection and pleasure
Love and fun we will always treasure

19 December 2016

Rose

How delicate the rose blooms
But what a pity that her beauty
Is often protected by thorns

1980s

Fragrant Rose

Petals of the rose endure
Palest colour soft and pure
Scent that draws us to be near
Fragrance fills our hearts so dear

Delicate buds unfurl their petals
Capture gaze that easily settles
Blooms that give such joy to others
Gifts of love to friends and mothers

3 August 2017

<u>Swallows</u>

You lift my spirit as you fly
Your speed of turn so graceful

I feel the air as you pass
So low and so skilful

You twist and turn and then alight
Chattering on the wire

Oh what delight blue wings long tail
You raise my spirit higher

June   2017

Mountain

You stand so high above the town
Your beauty capped by snowy crown
Sunlight wakes your craggy peaks
Faith and light for those who seek

29 July 2017

Inspired by Mt. Kazbek in Georgia

Cats Protection

Sitting on my lap you purr
Contentment when I stroke your fur
Trust that builds from day to day
Learning each other's words and ways

3 August 2017

Kingston to Houns Tout

We walk along the woodland way
Shielded from the heat of day
Overhead the bright green leaves
Filter light between the trees

Over the stile and across the grass
A few other walkers smile as they pass
Cows gently graze without a sound
Butterflies flutter and Wheatear abound

Open views of coast and farm
Splendour, peace and natural charm
Reaching the seat high above the sea
Calm waters glisten, open and free

11 August 2017

Bow Lake

Mountain covered in pure snow
Frozen lake lies still below

Spring thaw melts the frozen ice
Cracks announce each slow release

Sun is shining overhead
Crystal waters, colourful bed

No breeze to stir the icy water
Tranquil image will not alter

Reflected beauty, snowy peak
Natural haven of pure peace

14 August 2017

Inspired by Bow Lake, Alberta, Canada